INDIAN DESIGN

daab

Architects / Designers	Location	Page

INTRODUCTION, INSPIRATION SOURCES

BETWEEN TRADITION AND INNOVATION

India is diverse, multilayered, and rich in traditions with a past still passing by. Today India is able to maintain a ritualistic link with the heritage of the skilled craftsmanship, the remarkable presence of the past and the modern building process used; a high quality building stone and other traditional materials. Reflecting both the "old" and the "new"; and extending out into Bollywood, one of the most known areas to have adapted this.

The contemporary Indian design of today would not have being able to exist without the traditional one; as it is distinguished from the autonomous traditions of its ancient Hindu and Buddhist past.

It is now a built expression of an interaction between a global culture, the place and past, constantly changing; and becoming part of the 21st century, the "Mecca of the Software Revolution", one of the fastest growing economies in the world; with e-mail replacing the postman and a mobile phone becoming easier than a traditional one.

This volume at hand, then opens up a new dialogue between tradition and innovation, between craftsmanship and design and bringing both together to form what is now the contemporary design of India. Paying close attention to climate, flora, light, space, and material, to create a crafted space that adds richer texture and allows it to adapt a deeper meaning into the space, focusing on the essential, minimalist by heart and mood by its soul, being more than an aesthetic tool, instead meaningful.

Contemporary Indian design is then born out of its cultural influences of its time and place to become the reference of its own culture. As a result, creating a crafted environment that speaks of a journey in time and space.

ZWISCHEN TRADITION UND INNOVATION

Indien befindet sich in einem historischen Umbruch. Der Subkontinent mit seiner Milliardenbevölkerung, größter Armut und großem Reichtum blickt motiviert nach vorne ohne dabei jedoch seine kulturellen Wurzeln zu verlieren.

Besonders augenscheinlich ist das in der Architektur und im Design. Wie das vorliegende Buch eindrucksvoll zeigt, gelingt den Kreativen des Landes der Spagat zwischen High-Tech und traditioneller Handwerkskunst mit einer nahezu traumwandlerischer Sicherheit. Was zu einem großen Teil an den religiösen Riten und deren Einfluss auf Gestaltungsfragen liegt. Der Umgang mit Materialen, Ornamentik und vor allem Farben hat so gut wie immer eine spielerische Komponente, manchmal ist er geradezu enthusiastisch. Der unverkrampfte Mix aus alt und neu, aus modernem, internationalem Lebensstil und folkloristischer Tradition spiegelt sich in seiner Zuspitzung in der indischen Filmindustrie in Bollywood, deren Schmalz- und Tränendrüsen-Dramen längst vom Kitsch zum Kult avanciert sind. Genau dieser emotionale Mythos ist es, der auch seine Wellen in die indische Designszene hinein schlägt. Aber nicht nur dorthin. Blicken wir in die Welt der schnelllebigen Kreationen der Mode, so entdecken wir auch dort ganz deutlich den Einfluss dieser spirituell anmutenden Schaffenskraft.

Zeitgenössisches Indisches Design ist deshalb nur vor dem Hintergrund der Traditionen zu begreifen, die sich aus dem Hinduismus aber auch aus dem Buddhismus heraus entwickelt haben. Heute ist die spezifische indische Gestaltung Ausdruck einer Interaktion zwischen Globalität und technischem Fortschritt – extrem verkörpert im Mekka der Software Revolution in Bangalore – und der ausgeprägten, immer noch altertümlich erscheinenden Handwerkskunst.

Zur Verdeutlichung dieses essentiellen Wechselspiels startet das Buch mit „Inspiration Sources", den Quellen zur Ideenfindung. Dies ist eine kleine, optische Reise in die Traditionen der Schnitzkunst, Ornamentik, Farb- und Formgebung. Die weiteren, knapp fünfzig präsentierten Beispiele aus privatem Wohnen, öffentlichen Räumen, Hotels, Restaurants, Bars, Clubs, Läden und aus der Arbeitswelt bauen darauf auf und zeigen eine fein abgestimmte Mischung von Klassikern, über gelungene Kombinationen aus neu und alt bis hin zu minimalistischen Interieurs der jüngsten Zeit.

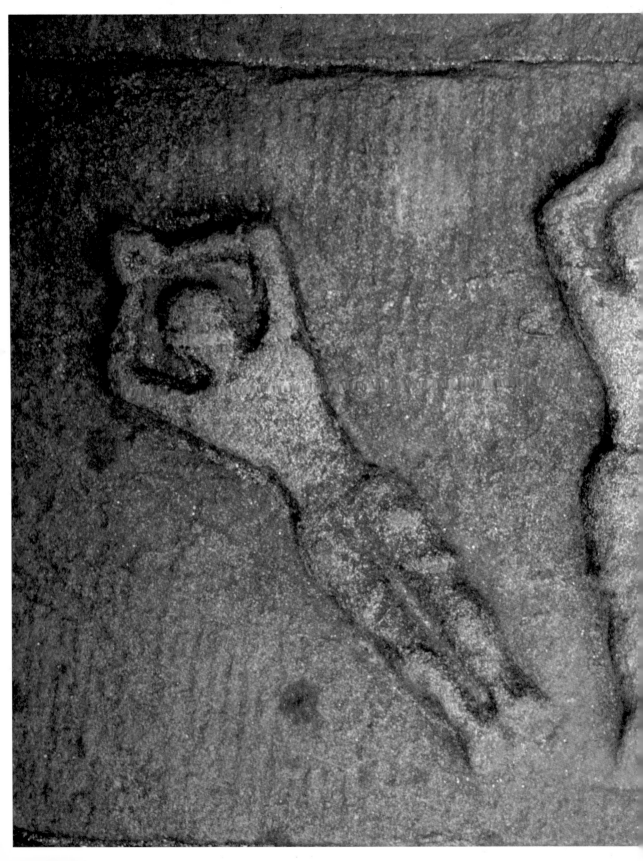

ENTRE TRADITION ET INNOVATION

L'Inde se trouve dans une période de bouleversement historique. Avec sa population d'un milliard d'habitant, sa très grande pauvreté et sa grande richesse, le sous-continent regarde avec motivation vers l'avant, sans toutefois perdre ses racines culturelles.

Ceci est particulièrement visible en architecture et en design. Comme le présent livre le montre de manière impressionnante, les créatifs du pays réussissent à faire la liaison entre high-tech et artisanat traditionnel quasiment avec la sûreté d'un somnambule, ceci étant en grande partie imputable aux rites religieux et à l'influence exercée par ceux-ci sur les questions d'aménagement. Le rapport avec les matériaux, les ornements et surtout les couleurs présente pratiquement toujours une composante ludique, il est parfois carrément plein d'enthousiasme. Le mélange non crispé d'ancien et de neuf, de style moderne, international et de tradition folklorique se reflète dans son aggravation au sein de l'industrie cinématographique indienne à Hollywood, dont les drames sentimentaux et larmoyants ont effectué depuis longtemps une avancée du kitsch au culte. C'est exactement ce mythe émotionnel qui répercute également ses ondes dans la scène du design indien. Mais pas uniquement là-bas. Si nous jetons un regard dans le monde des créations éphémères de la mode, nous y découvrons aussi de manière bien distincte l'influence de cette force de création d'impression spirituelle.

Le design indien contemporain ne peut être compris pour cette raison qu'en s'appuyant sur les traditions qui se sont développées de l'hindouisme mais aussi du bouddhisme. Aujourd'hui, l'aménagement indien spécifique est l'expression d'une interaction entre mondialisme et progrès technique, incarné de manière extrême à la Mecque de la révolution du logiciel à Bangalore, et dans l'artisanat marqué, d'apparence encore antique.

Pour élucider ce jeu d'échanges essentiel, le livre commence par le chapitre « Inspiration Sources », les sources de l'inspiration. Celui-ci est un petit voyage optique dans les traditions de la sculpture sur bois, de la technique ornementale, du façonnage et de la coloration. La cinquantaine d'autres exemples présentés d'appartement privés, de locaux publics, d'hôtels, de restaurants, de bars, de clubs, de magasins et tirés du monde du travail s'appuient dessus et montrent un fin mélange des classiques, via par une combinaison réussie du neuf et de l'ancien, jusqu'à des intérieurs minimalistes de l'époque récente.

ENTRE LA TRADICIÓN Y LA INNOVACIÓN

India con un pasado presente hoy en día, es capaz de mantener su conexión ritual con el patrimonio de la destreza, la presencia notable de su pasado y el proceso moderno de construcción aplicada; piedra de alta calidad y otros materiales tradicionales. Reflejando ambas épocas, la "vieja" y "nueva"; y de la misma manera, extendiéndose hacia Bollywood, una de las áreas más populares que ha llegado a seguir estos pasos.

El diseño con temporal de hoy en día en India no existiría sin el tradicional; el cual es distinguido de la tradición autónoma de su pasado ancestral hindú y budista. Presentándose ahora como una expresión interactiva entre la cultura global, el lugar y el pasado que la constituyen. En un cambio continuo que toma parte del siglo 21, el "Meca de la Revolución del Software", una de las economías de alto crecimiento en el mundo, con el correo electrónico reemplazando al cartero y el teléfono celular facilitando mas posibilidades que el usual.

Este volumen en mano presenta la posibilidad de abrir un nuevo dialogo entre lo tradicional y la innovación, entre la destreza y el diseño, combinando ambos para formar el diseño con temporal del India de ahora. Prestando atención al clima, flora, luz, espacio, y material, para crear un espacio detallado que adhiere riqueza en textura y permite la adaptación de un significado mas afondo hacia el espacio, enfocándose en lo esencial, y el minimalismo que le da un significado puro al espacio.

Es decir, que el diseño con temporal de India nace a través de sus influencias culturales, de su tiempo y ubicación, para convertirse en la referencia de su propia cultura; y como resultado, creando un ambiente detallado que habla de una jornada en tiempo y espacio.

TRA LA TRADIZIONE E L'INNOVAZIONE

L'India si trova ad una svolta storica. Il subcontinente con la sua popolazione di miliardi, la più grande povertà e le sue grandi ricchezze con motivazione punta lo sguardo in avanti, senza tuttavia perdere le sue radici culturali.

Ciò si evidenzia in modo particolare nell'architettura e nel design. Così come lo dimostra il presente volume in modo impressionante, i creativi del paese riescono a superare la spaccata tra l'high tech e l'arte artigianale tradizionale con la sicurezza dei sonnambuli, il ché è dovuto in gran parte ai riti religiosi e la loro influenza sulle creazioni. Il modo d'impiegare materiali, ornamenti e soprattutto colori ha quasi sempre una componente giocosa, a volte è addirittura entusiasmante. Questo mix disinvolto tra il vecchio ed il nuovo, lo stile di vita internazionale e la tradizione folcloristica si rispecchia e culmina nell'industria cinematografica indiana a Hollywood, i cui drammi di sentimentalismo e lacrime da tempo da kitsch sono diventati cult. Ed è proprio questo mito emozionante che butta le onde sulla scena indiana del design. Ma non soltanto lì. Se vogliamo dare uno sguardo nel mondo delle effimere creazioni della moda, scopriamo anche lì l'evidente influenza di questo potere creativo che sembra quasi spirituale.

Il design indiano contemporaneo si riesce pertanto a capire soltanto sul fondo delle tradizioni sviluppatesi dall'induismo, ma anche dal buddismo. Oggi le specifiche creazioni indiane sono l'espressione dell'interazione tra la globalità ed il progresso tecnologico – che si manifesta in modo estremo nel Mecca della rivoluzione del software a Bangalore – da una parte e l'arte artigianale spiccata che tuttavia ancora oggi ha l'aria dell'antiquato.

Per illustrare questo gioco alterno ed essenziale, il volume inizia con le „Inspiration Sources", le risorse dalle quali sgorgano le idee. Vuol essere un piccolo viaggio ottico verso le tradizioni dell'arte dell'intaglio, delle creazioni con ornamenti, dei colori e delle forme. I quasi cinquanta esempi seguenti di abitazioni private, locali pubblici, hotel, ristoranti, bar, club e negozi, nonché esempi dal mondo del lavoro sono basati su questi fondamenti e dimostrano un raffinato misto dal classico, attraverso riuscite combinazioni tra vecchio e nuovo fino ad arredi interni minimalistici dai tempi più recenti.

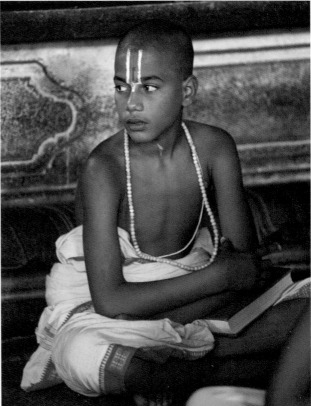

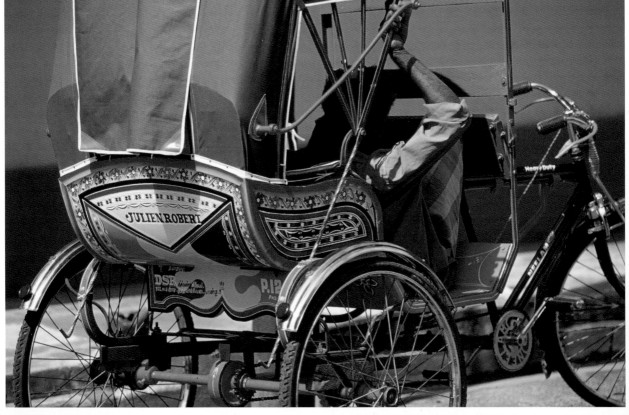

LIVING SPACES - PRIVATE HOUSES, APARTMENTS & LOFTS

4.4. DESIGN | DELHI
Nanda Residence
Private Living Space
Mumbai | 2000

LE CORBUSIER | FRANCE
Sarabhai House
Private Living Space
Ahmedabad | 1995

JOERG DRECHSEL | FORT COCHIN
Private Mansion
Private Living Space
Fort Cochin | 2002

DOMINIC DUBÉ | BANGALORE
Inge's House
Private Living Space
Auroville | 2002

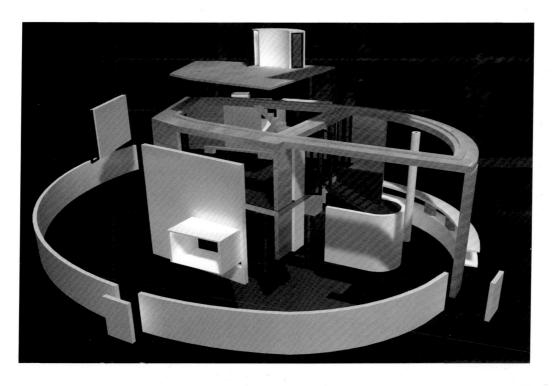

SANDEEP KHOSLA | BANGALORE
Manwaring House
Private Living Space
Bangalore | 2003

JEAN FRANCOIS LESAGE, VASTRA KALA | CHENNAI
Luz House
Private Living Space
Chennai | 1997

KAMAL MALIK ARCHITECTS | MUMBAI
Metha House
Private Living Spaces
Pune | 2002

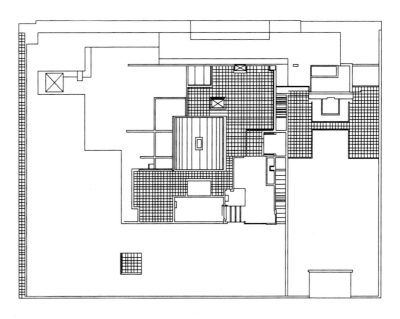

JITENDRA MISTRY, MISTRY ASSOCIATES | AHMEDABAD
Lalbhai Haveli
Private Living Space
Ahmedabad | 1997

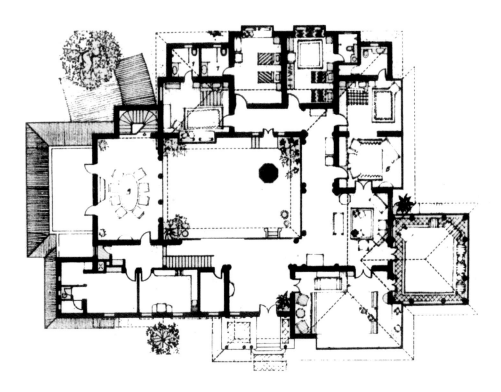

PINAKIN PATEL | ALIBAUG
Patel Residence
Private Living Space
Alibaug | 2001

VISALAKSHI RAMASWAMY, BENNY KURIAKOSE | CHENNAI
Visalakshi Ramamswamy Beach House
Private Living Space
Chennai | 2002

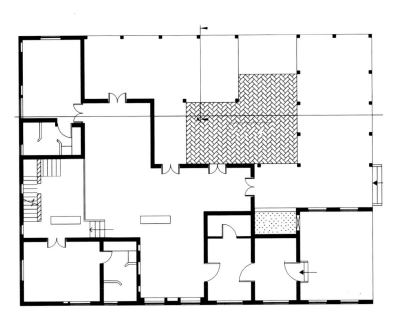

RAJIV SAINI + ASSOCIATES | MUMBAI
House B
Private Living Space
Delhi

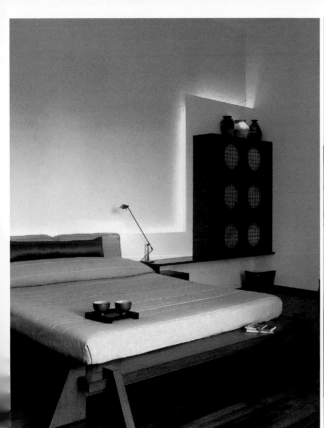

RAJIV SAINI + ASSOCIATES | MUMBAI
Apartment G
Private Living Space
Mumbai

SAMIRA RATHOD DESIGN ASSOCIATES | MUMBAI
Karjat House
Private Living Space
Karjat | 2003

J. CAMPBELL, D. E. GOSLING, SCOTT MCCLELLAND
David Sassoon Library
Public Space
Mumbai I 1870

CHARLES CORREA | MUMBAI
Kala Academy
Public Space
Goa | 1983

SOUMITRO GHOSH, MATHEW & GHOSH ARCHITECTS | BANGALORE
Bethel Baptist Church
Public Space
Bangalore | 2002

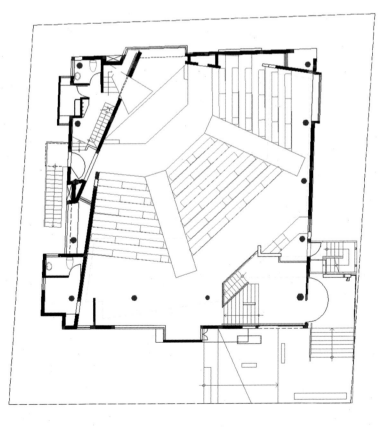

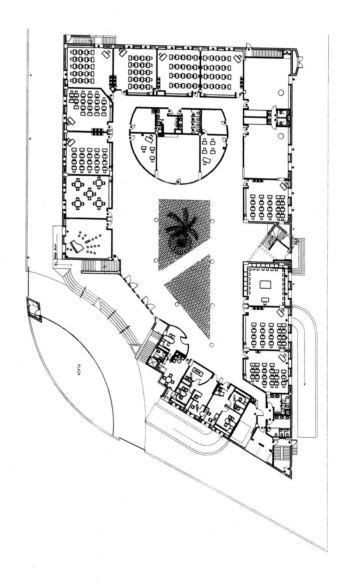

HOSPITALITY SPACES - HOTELS & RESORTS

HARI AJWANI, CLAUDIA DERIAN | GOA
Fort Tiracol
Hospitality Space
Goa | 2003

HARI AJWANI, CLAUDIA DERIAN | GOA
Nilaya Hermitage
Hospitality Space
Goa | 1995

SAMIRA RATHOD DESIGN ASSOCIATES | **MUMBAI**
The Asian Age Office
Working Space
Mumbai | 2002

INDEX

copyright © 2004 daab
cologne   london   new york

published and distributed worldwide by
daab gmbh
stadtwaldgürtel 57
d - 50935 köln

t +49-221-94 10 740
f +49-221-94 10 741

mail@daab-online.de
www.daab-online.de

publisher ralf daab
rdaab@daab-online.de

art director feyyaz
mail@feyyaz.com

editors
bharath ramamrutham & monika ghurde, chennai
dr sonal shah, mumbai
dagmar von tschurtschenthaler, munich

editorial project by fusion publishing gmbh stuttgart   los angeles
editorial direction martin nicholas kunz
editorial coordination gabriele fürst
copyright © 2004 fusion publishing, www.fusion-publishing.com

layout monika ghurde, chennai
imaging jan hausberg, käthe nennstiel, susanne olbrich

introduction joerg drechsel, cort cochin
german translation martin nicholas kunz
french translation ade team dominique santoro
spanish translation michelle galindo
italian translation ade team jacqueline rizzer

special thanks to hari ajwani & claudia derian, joerg drechsel as well as
ELLE DECOR india for their support and expert advise

printed in spain
Anman Gràfiques del Vallès, Spain
www.anman.com

isbn 3-937718-04-4
d.l.: B-41.025-04

GAUTAM BHATIA | NEW DELHI
NAVIN GUPTA | UDAIPUR
RAJIV SAINI | MUMBAI
Devi Garh
Hospitality Space
Udaipur| 2000

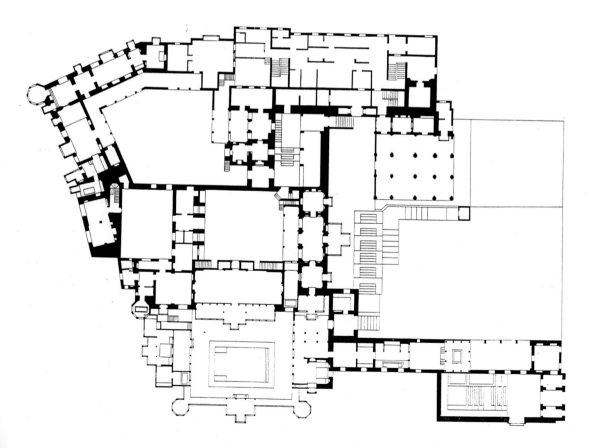

JOERG DRECHSEL | FORT COCHIN
Malabar Escape
Hospitality Space
Kerala | 2003

CONRAN DESIGN | LONDON
The Park Bangalore
Hospitality Space
Bangalore | 2002

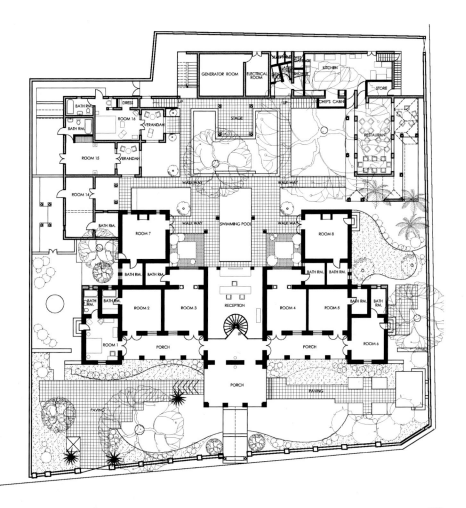

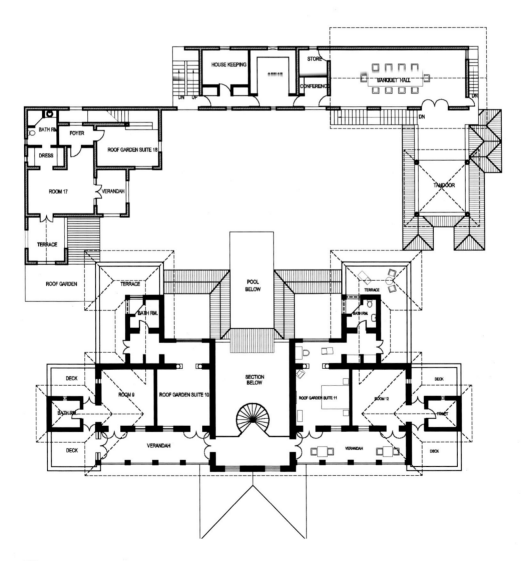

HOUSE KEEPING

STORE

CONFERENCE

BANQUET HALL

DN UP

DN

DN

BATH RM

FOYER

DRESS

ROOF GARDEN SUITE 18

TANDOOR

ROOM 17

VERANDAH

TERRACE

ROOF GARDEN

TERRACE

POOL BELOW

TERRACE

BATH RM.

BATH RM.

DECK

SECTION BELOW

DECK

ROOM 9

ROOF GARDEN SUITE 10

ROOF GARDEN SUITE 11

ROOM 12

BATH RM.

TOILET

DECK

VERANDAH

VERANDAH

DECK

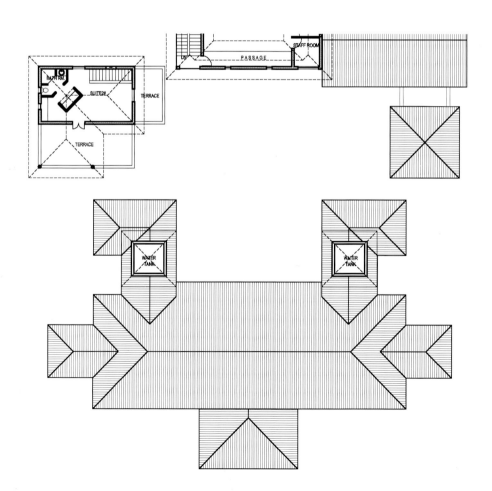

HIRSCH & BEDNER ASSOCIATES I LOS ANGELES
The Park Chennai
Hospitality Space
Chennai I 2003

UTE SCHUTZ, RAIMUND IMO | GOA
Raj Angan
Hospitality Space
Goa | 2004

PRATAP MALIK & ASSOCIATES I **DELHI**
AKSHAY KRAUL, PRATAB JYOTI
Shreyas /(Pawan/Leesha)
Hospitality Space
Bangalore I 2004

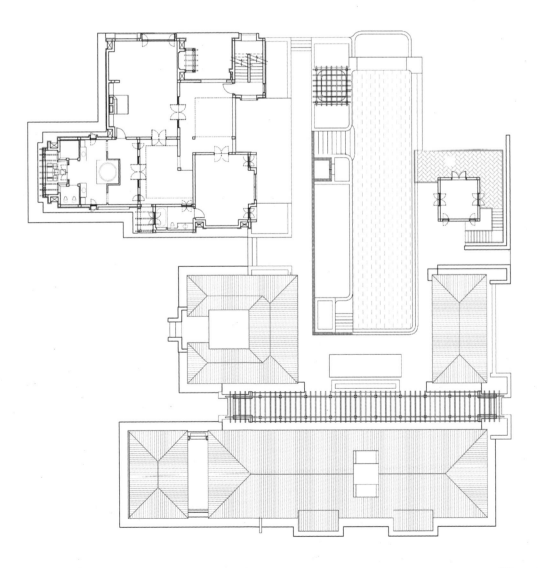

PRADEEP SACHDEVA DESIGN ASSOCIATES | NEW DELHI
Samode Haveli
Hospitality Space
Jaipur | 2003

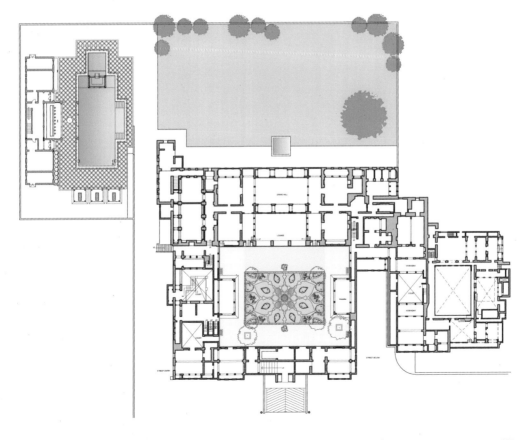

DENZIL SEQUIERA | GOA
Elsewhere
Hospitality Space
Goa | 2003

MAHARAWAL LAXMAN SINGHJI & MAHARAWAL UDAI SINGHJI
M.K. HARSHVARDHAN SINGH | DUNGARPUR
Udai Bilas Palace
Hospitality Space
Dungarpur | 1940

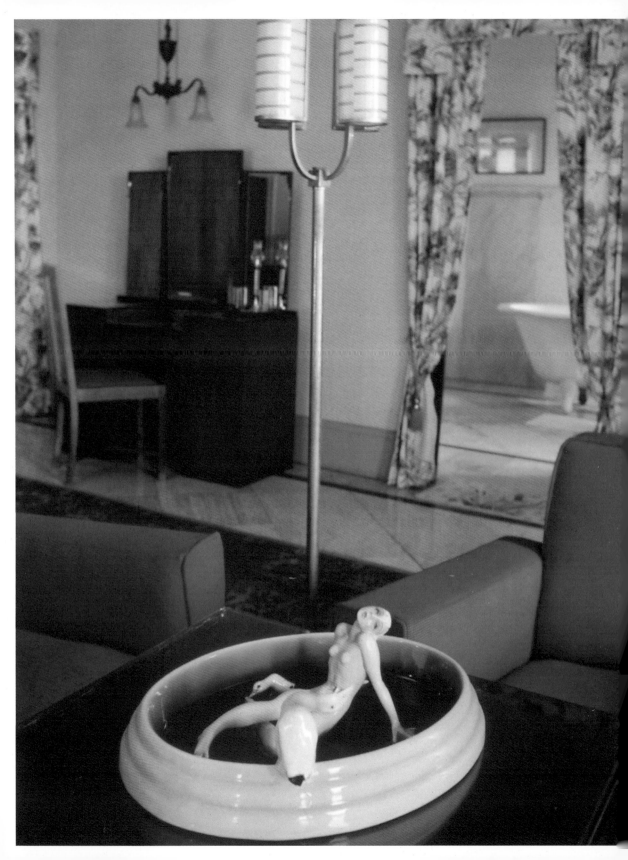

VARUN SOOD | GOA
Siolim House
Hospitality Space
Goa | 1999

LEISURE SPACES - RESTAURANTS, BARS & LOUNGES

RAHUL AKBERBAR | MUMBAI
Indigo
Leisure Space
Restaurant & Bar
Mumbai | 2002

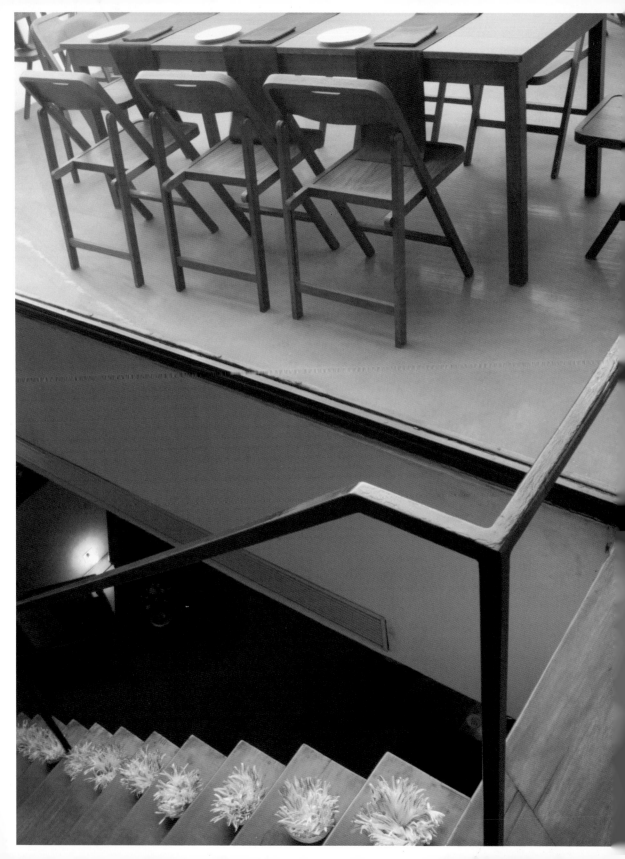

DBA DESIGNPHASE PTE. LTD, SHAFEE SAJARI | SINGAPORE
Insomnia at the Taj Mahal Palace Mumbai
Leisure Space
Night Club & Discotheque
Mumbai | 2002

DBA DESIGNPHASE PTE. LTD, SHAFEE SAJARI | SINGAPORE
Souk at the Taj Mahal Palace Mumbai
Leisure Space
Restaurant
Mumbai | 2002

HIRSCH, BEDNER & ASSOCIATES | LOS ANGELES
Pasha
Leisure Space
Club & Bar Lounge
Chennai | 2003

SANDEEP KHOSLA ASSOCIATES | BANGALORE
Spin
Leisure Space
Club & Lounge Bar
Bangalore | 2003

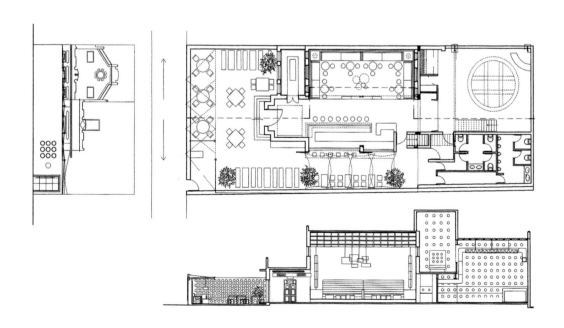

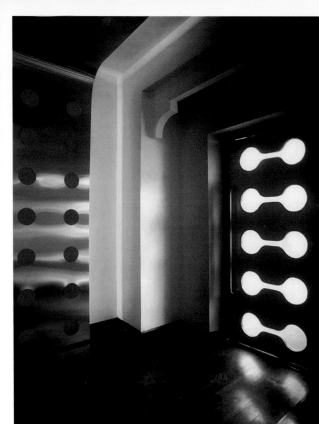

WENDELL RODRICKS | GOA
Ozone
Leisure Space
Restaurant & Bar
Goa | 2001

OZONE

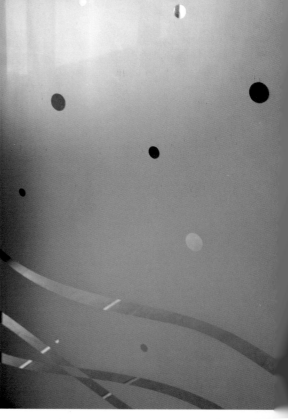

RAJIV SAINI + ASSOCIATES I MUMBAI
Senso
Restaurant & Bar
Delhi I 2002

RAJIV SAINI + ASSOCIATES | MUMBAI
Velvet Lounge
Leisure Space
Lounge
Delhi | 2002

RAJIV SAINI + ASSOCIATES | MUMBAI
Rain
Leisure Spaces
Restaurant & Bar
Mumbai | 2002

RETAIL SPACES - SHOWROOMS & SHOPS

ANDREA ANASTASIO | BANGALORE
Cinnamon
Retail Space
Bangalore | 1999

PAUSE

BRAND NEW DAY | BANGALORE
DOMINIC DUBÉ, ABHISHEK PODDAR
Pause
Retail Space
Bangalore | 2004

PAUSE

INTERSPACE INC | CHENNAI
VIKRAM PHADKE
Evoluzione Design Center
Retail Space
Chennai | 2003

RAJIV SAINI + ASSOCIATES | MUMBAI
Karma
Retail Space
Delhi

SOUMITRO GOSH, ABHISHEK PODDAR | BANGALORE
Cinnamon
Retail Space
Fort Cochin | 2002

HARI AJWANI, CLAUDIA DERIAN | GOA
Sangolda
Retail Space
Goa | 1999

WORKING SPACES - CORPORATE BUILDINGS & INTERIORS

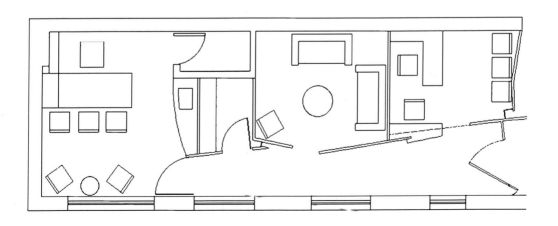

KHOSLA ASSOCIATES & TSK DESIGN | BANGALORE
SANDEEP KHOSLA, TANIA SINGH KOSLA
MTV Office
Working Space
Bangalore | 1998

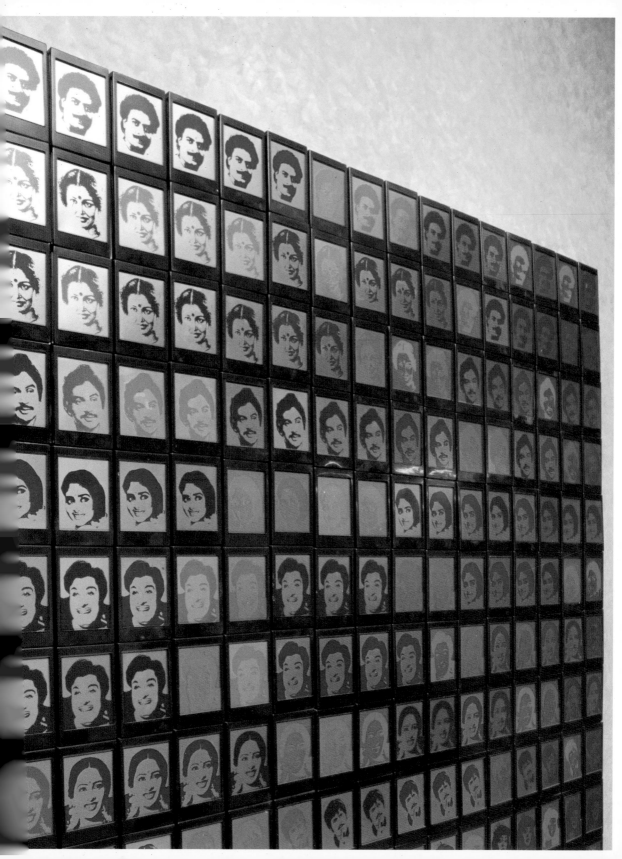

KAMAL MALIK ARCHITECTS | MUMBAI
Lupin Laboratories
Working Space
Pune | 2001